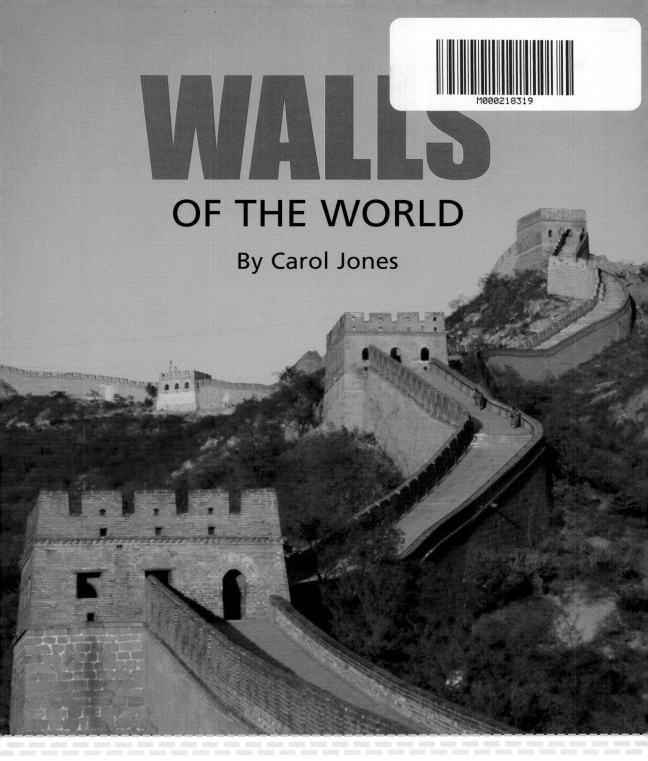

WALLS
OF THE WORLD

By Carol Jones

CELEBRATION PRESS
Pearson Learning Group

The following people from **Pearson Learning Group**
have contributed to the development of this product:

Joan Mazzeo, Dorothea Fox **Design** | **Editorial** Leslie Feierstone-Barna, Terri Crawford Jones
Christine Fleming **Marketing** | **Publishing Operations** Jennifer Van Der Heide
Production Laura Benford-Sullivan
Content Area Consultant Dr. Daniel J. Gelo

The following people from **DK** have
contributed to the development of this product:

Art Director Rachael Foster
Martin Wilson **Managing Art Editor** | **Managing Editor** Marie Greenwood
Clair Watson **Design** | **Editorial** Marian Broderick
Brenda Clynch **Picture Research** | **Production** Gordana Simakovic
Richard Czapnik, Andy Smith **Cover Design** | **DTP** David McDonald
Consultant Philip Wilkinson

Dorling Kindersley would like to thank: Peter Bull for original artwork, Sarah Nunan for additional design, Lucy Heaver and Julie Ferris for editorial help. Rose Horridge, Gemma Woodward, and Hayley Smith in the DK Picture Library. Johnny Pau for additional cover design work.

Picture Credits: AKG London: 13t, 27; Erich Lessing 23tr. Bridgeman Art Library, London/New York: Giraudon 15tr. Corbis: David Ball 6; Bettmann 26, 28t, 29tr; Bennett Dean/Eye Ubiquitous 10b; Dallas and John Heaton/ 1; Chris Hellier 15b; Colin Hoskins/Cordaiy Photo Library Ltd. 19tr; Dave G. Houser 21; MIT Collection 18-19b; David Reed 18tr; Keren Su 8-9; David Turnley 3; Peter Turnley 30; Patrick Ward 24tl; Adam Woolfitt 23b. Werner Forman Archive: 14tl. Sonia Halliday Photographs: F.H.C. Birch 12. Hutchison Library: J.Egan 20b. ImageState/Pictor: 5t, 11b, 17b. Rex Features: Sipa Press 29b. World Pictures: 7br, 32; l. Roussillon 4. Jacket: Corbis: Peter Turnley back. Masterfile UK: Miles Ertman front t.

All other images: Dorling Kindersley © 2005. For further information see www.dkimages.com

ISBN: 0-7652-5260-0

Color reproduction by Colourscan, Singapore
Printed in the United States of America
2 3 4 5 6 7 8 9 10   08 07 06 05

1-800-321-3106
www.pearsonlearning.com

Contents

Amazing Walls

Perched high on a hilltop in France, the ancient city of Carcassonne looks like it jumped off the pages of a book of tales about kings and queens and knights in armor. Carcassonne is considered Europe's finest medieval walled city. Its walls, with fifty-two stone towers, were built about 1,000 years ago. It is just one example of amazing walls that people have built throughout history.

Some walls are very old. It's hard to imagine that a wall built today could still be standing after 1,000 years. Walls can also be extraordinary because of their size. The Great Wall of China runs thousands of miles across mountains and valleys. Walls can be extremely strong, strikingly beautiful, or precisely constructed. If you study any wall closely enough, you will find something amazing about it.

The medieval part of Carcassonne, France, is encircled by ancient walls, while the modern city lies outside.

Many different materials have been and are used to build walls. People used earth to build some of the earliest known fort walls. Sometimes earth was packed into a wooden frame to construct a wall. The frame held the earth in place.

People constructed longer-lasting **masonry** walls from brick or stone. They put the bricks or stones together with **mortar**, a cement-like substance. The mortar holds the bricks or stones in place and fills any small gaps or cracks to make a solid wall. Some highly skilled stonecutters could make blocks that did not require mortar. For example, builders of the city of Great Zimbabwe cut each stone to fit so perfectly that no mortar was needed to hold the stones in place.

a section of the walls of Great Zimbabwe

The ancient Romans used concrete for construction. Concrete is still used today because it is inexpensive, strong, and can be molded into many different shapes.

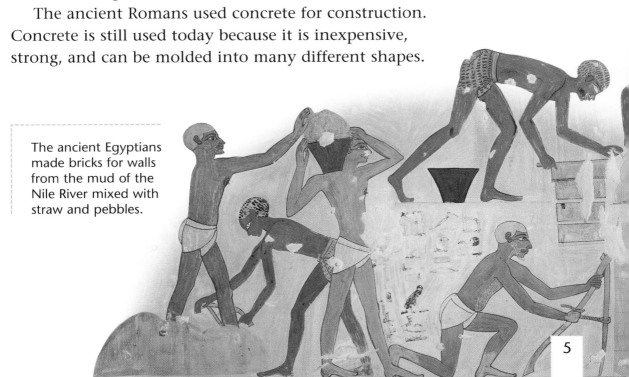

The ancient Egyptians made bricks for walls from the mud of the Nile River mixed with straw and pebbles.

Once a wall was built, the work was not always over. Walls built for protection had to be patrolled to be sure that no one tried to climb over them or knock them down.

The Roman builders of Hadrian's Wall in England designed their wall so that soldiers could patrol from the top. Being so high up, they could spot intruders far in the distance. Outer layers of cut stone, called **facings**, covered a core of rocks, rubble, cement, and clay. Soldiers on the top of the wall were protected by a low wall, or **parapet**.

In this book, you can read about six amazing walls. Two were built for protection from attacking enemies. Two were built to symbolize, or stand for, something. Two were built to mark a boundary. No matter what the material, design, or purpose, all the walls in this book have a story to tell.

From the top of Hadrian's Wall, Roman soldiers could spot hostile groups from the north.

Walls That Protect

The best walls built to protect a city or an area were made high and wide. The thicker and higher a wall was, the harder it would be for enemies to destroy. Constantinople's walls were so huge that they protected the city for 1,000 years.

Another advantage of thick walls was that people could walk on top of them. Soldiers stationed on top of the Great Wall of China kept watch over the countryside for a great distance.

Great Wall of China

Like an immense sleeping dragon, the Great Wall of China has protected the northern border of China for more than 2,000 years. Winding over mountains and across deserts, the Great Wall of China is the longest wall ever built. Although parts of it have crumbled or disappeared, it stretches almost 4,000 miles from Po Hai on the Yellow Sea far into the deserts of Central Asia. However, it was not built all at once, and it has changed from its earliest form.

Mongolia

Great Wall

China

The Great Wall of China

Many additions were made to the Great Wall of China over the centuries.

Many centuries ago, China was made up of several kingdoms. These kingdoms built walls around their land to protect themselves from their unfriendly neighbors. In the third century B.C., the Qin **dynasty** conquered the other kingdoms, creating one large kingdom. The **emperor** of the Qin empire, Shi Huangdi, ordered the walls to be united, building new sections as needed. Thousands of workers worked for many years to create the wall. One new wall was built to protect the **empire** from northern invaders.

The Great Wall's height—23 to 26 feet—worked well as a protection against invaders. Its width—19 feet—made it a good roadway for troops and horses.

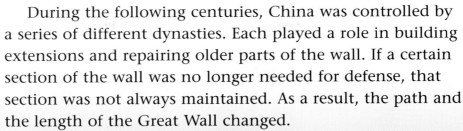

During the following centuries, China was controlled by a series of different dynasties. Each played a role in building extensions and repairing older parts of the wall. If a certain section of the wall was no longer needed for defense, that section was not always maintained. As a result, the path and the length of the Great Wall changed.

Most of the wall that stands today was constructed during the Ming dynasty (1368–1644). During this period, the wall was made longer and stronger to keep out northern groups, such as the Manchus. Even with the wall as protection, the Manchus defeated the Ming in 1644. Their dynasty lasted until 1912. During this dynasty, the wall lost its importance as a defensive weapon, and it slowly fell into ruin.

Building the Great Wall

The wall was built with materials found in the area. On the steep mountainsides, layers of soil were packed into wooden frames to form the wall.

In the sandy soil of the Gobi Desert in western China, the wall was built mainly of gravel, sand, and water. These materials were mixed with reeds and twigs and packed firmly into wooden frames. This mixture dried rock-hard with the reeds and twigs reinforcing the building blocks, like steel rods do in modern-day concrete.

In the fourteenth century, the Ming dynasty used stone blocks for the **foundation** and earth for the core of the wall. The outside was covered with kiln-fired bricks and stone slabs. Bricks paved the top of the wall, forming a solid roadway for horses and men.

two layers of brick

layers of stones, rubble, and earth

facings

Materials making up the inside of the Great Wall became finer as the wall increased in height.

Gaps in the parapet of the Great Wall allowed the Chinese soldiers to keep watch.

Life on the Great Wall

Once the Great Wall was completed, the Chinese warriors held a great advantage over their enemies to the north. Soldiers and horses could move freely and quickly on top of the wall over treacherous mountain passes. Watchtowers, tall towers spaced along the wall, served as lookout points for soldiers to scan the horizon for invaders.

The Great Wall was also the soldiers' home. Living quarters were inside the watchtowers, along with storerooms for food and weapons. Baskets of supplies were hauled by rope to the top of the wall.

Although the Great Wall benefited China, it was built at a tremendous cost in human suffering. Beginning with the Qin dynasty, each ruler used slaves to build the wall. In addition, peasants and criminals were forced to work as laborers. Many of them died working on the wall. Sometimes their bodies were buried in the wall itself.

Today, the Great Wall no longer guards against invaders. Tourists—not soldiers—walk the roadways. The wall has become a symbol of the might of an ancient civilization.

The Great Wall of China is one of the country's most visited tourist sites.

Istanbul's Theodosian Walls

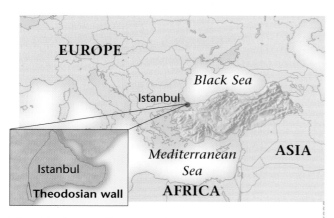

Theodosian walls around Constantinople (present-day Istanbul)

For centuries, the city of Istanbul, Turkey, has been the gateway between Europe and Asia. Once called Byzantium, the city was renamed Constantinople in A.D. 330 after the Roman emperor Constantine. It was the richest city in the Christian world. Surrounded by sea on three sides, Constantinople was a natural fort. In the fifth century A.D., Roman emperor Theodosius II ordered the construction of double walls to surround the city. Although some of the land wall is still standing, most of the sea wall is gone. The wall must have been a daunting sight to an invading army. The first thing attackers would see was a double set of walls soaring 30 feet into the air. Arrows shot by archers from behind the thick walls would rain down upon them.

These crumbling remains of the Theodosian walls show the inner wall, the outer wall, and the watchtowers.

Then the attackers would see the gaping **moat** full of murky water. They would find that they were too far away for their arrows or guns to do any damage to the wall.

In the fifth century, the Roman empire was fading, and its territory was shrinking. By A.D. 410, Rome itself was being attacked. Only in the East was the empire's strength intact. This eastern empire became known as the Byzantine empire, with Constantinople as its capital. Theodosius II came into power in A.D. 408. He knew that the empire had many enemies who would love to conquer the rich and centrally located city, so he decided to build walls around it.

Constantinople in the 1490s, after its conquest by the Ottomans

Constantinople was located on a peninsula, which meant that it was protected by water on three sides. Invaders would most likely come across the land. So in A.D. 412, the first set of walls went up across the peninsula. To this land barrier, Theodosius II added sea walls, which ran all the way around the city. Constantinople was now completely surrounded. The walls protected the city from many attacks over the next 1,000 years. Crusaders from Europe occupied the city for some time during the thirteenth century, however, it wasn't until 1453 that an invader—the Ottoman Turks—finally conquered the city. The name of the city was changed to Istanbul.

Building the Walls

Constantinople's land walls were a complete system. They included an inner, or main, wall and an outer wall, with a road between the two for moving troops. Outside the walls was a wide moat, which prevented enemies from bringing their cannons or catapults close enough to do any damage. Soldiers were posted at 11 fortified gates and 192 towers. Each tower of the outer wall was positioned, or staggered, between two towers of the main wall to present a solid line of defense.

Some of the fortified gates in the wall have fallen into disuse.

The builders used layers of thin red bricks, facings of larger blocks of cream-colored limestone, and a rubble core to construct the wall. Rubble is a mix of small rocks, gravel, and broken bricks. The outer layer of bricks helped stiffen the walls and strengthen the bond between the rubble core and the limestone facings.

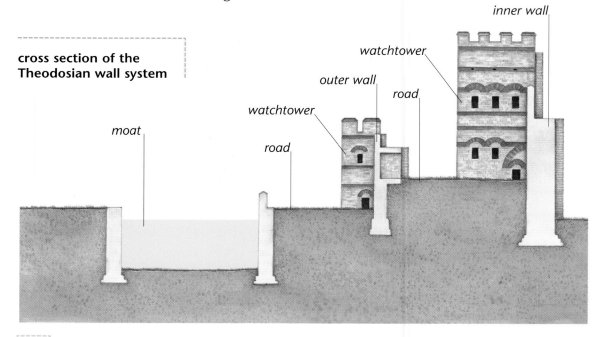

cross section of the Theodosian wall system

moat

road

watchtower

outer wall

road

watchtower

inner wall

The builders began by creating facings seven to eleven limestone blocks high. They put the blocks together with mortar. These facings were filled with a core of rubble. Then, builders set five layers of bricks across the entire surface. This process was repeated until the walls reached the height they wanted them to be.

In the years that followed the construction, there were many attacks on the walls. However, with such a good method of defense, the city leaders had few worries. As other parts of the Byzantine empire were lost to invaders and conquerors, the walls of Constantinople ensured that the city remained the center of Byzantine civilization for many years.

Although large sections of the walls have since disappeared or crumbled, the Turkish government has restored some of the sections still standing to their former glory. Cars now zip through the gates, and tourists come to admire the walls, an impressive reminder of the once-powerful Byzantine empire.

The wall protected Constantinople's artistic treasures, such as this fifth-century mosaic of a peasant.

A modern reconstruction brings the inner wall back to its original size— 30 feet high and 16 feet thick.

Walls as Symbols

While some walls have been built to protect cities and lands, other walls have been constructed to represent an idea or to remember a time in history. Unlike Constantinople's walls, the walls of Great Zimbabwe in Africa were a symbol of wealth and importance. The Vietnam Veterans Memorial wall in Washington, D.C. remembers people who died in war.

Great Zimbabwe

Great Zimbabwe in present-day Zimbabwe

Great Zimbabwe

In 1871, a German explorer, Carl Mauch, was making his way across a field in south-central Africa. Ahead of him he saw a green hill with patches of bare rock. As he drew closer, he realized that the bare rock was ruins of stone buildings and walls. Before him stood a great tower made of granite blocks. He assumed the ruins belonged to a lost city built by the Queen of Sheba. Later research proved that these great walls were built between the twelfth and fifteenth centuries by the ancestors of Africa's Bantu-speaking Shona people.

The ruins are what is left of a city called Great Zimbabwe, which was once home to more than 10,000 people. The center of the town was a group of stone-wall enclosures set high upon a hill, referred to as the Hill Complex. One of these enclosures was a temple. The others enclosed dwellings of the town's most important citizens. Below the hill is a large circular stone wall, called the Great Enclosure. Inside this wall are several other smaller enclosures that belonged to the king's family and an enormous tower that stands over 30 feet high.

The early people of this region grew crops and raised livestock. Later, they learned how to mine for gold. By the ninth century, Great Zimbabwe had become an important center for trade in metals and other goods. As a result, some of the townspeople grew very rich. By the eleventh century, a class system had developed. The people of the rich upper classes began building walls around their dwellings, while the poor lower classes lived in small, round huts outside the wall. The walls clearly showed that, although poor people had to live crowded together, the rich enjoyed the luxury of space and privacy and used the walls to display their power.

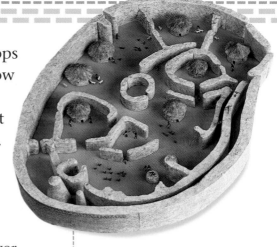

An upper-class family and their servants lived in the round huts within this enclosure.

the stone ruins of Great Zimbabwe

Building the Walls

The largest wall ruin in the area is the Great Enclosure. Its walls are 800 feet long, 16 feet thick, and 32 feet high. The granite facings are filled with rubble and stones. Workers cut nearly one million granite stones to make just this one wall.

Although this was a great deal of work, the granite rocks in this area were easy to split. The combination of hot days and cold nights would often cause the rocks to split naturally. They would expand in the heat and contract in the cold. This constant expanding and shrinking caused tiny cracks in the rocks to grow larger. Finally, the rocks would split along the cracks.

To speed up this process, stonecutters would light fires on the rocks and then pour cold water on them. Another method they used was to hammer wedges into the cracks to split the rocks into slabs.

This solid cone-shaped tower has an inner core of rubble.

Stonecutters used hammers and chisels to shape slabs of granite into small, smooth blocks. The blocks were so smooth and perfectly shaped that no mortar was needed. The stonecutters also created patterns in the walls by using blocks of different colors and textures.

Talented stonecutters created strong, beautiful walls.

After the fifteenth century, the city of Great Zimbabwe was abandoned. The people may have left because of a war or perhaps because the farmland around the city could no longer support them. Over time, Great Zimbabwe was forgotten to all except those people who lived nearby. **Archaeologists** hope that they can uncover more secrets of this once great city.

the remains of Great Zimbabwe

Vietnam Veterans Memorial

Vietnam Veterans Memorial in Washington, D.C.

In a grassy park in Washington, D.C. stands a wall of black granite. The names of nearly 60,000 people are carved in the polished surface of the wall. Unlike other walls, this wall is not designed to contain anything. Rather, it is a symbol of respect for U.S. **citizens** who are still missing or who died in the Vietnam War.

The United States first sent troops to Vietnam in 1961. Over the next fourteen years, U.S. citizens disagreed bitterly over the war in Vietnam. Many people felt that the government should stop the fighting. Others believed that the United States had a duty to stay and fight. The government finally decided to bring its soldiers home in 1975.

Soldiers returning from Vietnam were not treated like heroes. Instead, the confusion and anger many people felt about the war was directed toward the returning soldiers. Many people simply wanted to forget about the war as quickly as possible. Although veterans of other wars had been honored with **monuments**, little was done for Vietnam veterans.

Visitors leave flowers, wreaths and other mementos to honor those named on the Vietnam Veterans Memorial.

Starting in 1979, a group of people raised money to build a memorial to honor all the U.S. citizens who died in the war. A national competition was held for the design. Maya Lin, an architectural student at Yale University, submitted the winning design for the memorial.

Building the Wall

The simple design called for a 493-foot-long V-shaped wall of polished black granite. The names of almost 60,000 men and women are carved in the granite. The back of the wall was set into a groove in the earth.

Construction began in March 1982 in a park in Washington, D.C. Black granite slabs were cut in India. The slabs were polished to make them smooth and shiny, and then the names were chiseled into the stone. The project took only eight months to complete.

This design was chosen because the wall represents a boundary between the living and the dead. The black granite gives a feeling of sadness and seriousness. The shiny surface reflects the sky, the sun, and the faces of all who come to pay their respects to those who did not return.

Visitors to the Vietnam Veterans Memorial can walk along its full length.

Walls That Mark Borders

Some walls have been built to mark a boundary and to separate two places. Hadrian's Wall was built across England from coast to coast to separate Roman-held territory from the lands to the north. In the city of Berlin, a wall was built to surround and separate the western part of the city that was governed by democratic West Germany from communist East Germany.

Hadrian's Wall

Hadrian's Wall in England

Hadrian's Wall lies in ruins today, but about 1,800 years ago it was an amazing sight. Like the walls of Constantinople, it was a military zone. It included a thick, high wall fronted by a deep ditch on the north side and punctuated by small forts and lookout towers. The stone wall was 73 miles long, 15 feet high, and its width ranged from 6 to 10 feet. It also had a second earthen wall and ditch, called a **vallum**, which ran along the south side of the stone wall.

Small forts were placed every Roman mile, or 615 feet. They are called mile castles for this reason. Each of these mile castles housed about fifty soldiers. The soldiers' job was to keep track of who passed through the gates in the mile castles. Turrets were also built on the wall, two between each mile castle. Every small lookout tower housed between four and eight soldiers who kept watch over the land. Sixteen large forts were also built near the wall. They each housed between 500 and 1,000 soldiers.

Hadrian became emperor of the Roman empire in A.D. 117. He **inherited** a great empire and ruled over captured lands that extended into Turkey, the Middle East, the northern edge of Africa, and much of Europe and England.

When the Romans tried to take over the north of England, they found that the people there did not give in easily. When Hadrian became emperor, he chose not to try to expand the empire any farther north. He decided to build a wall to separate the Roman territory from the fierce peoples in the north instead. Unlike the walls of Constantinople, the main purpose of this wall was to control who came and went. The only way in and out was through patrolled gates.

Hadrian
(A.D. 76–138)

Hadrian's Wall marked the northern edge of the Roman Empire in England.

23

Building the Wall

Hadrian's Wall was built by Roman soldiers. They worked for six years to complete it. Hadrian's plans called for a wall 10 feet wide with stone facings and a core of rubble and cement. About 23 miles of the wall followed this plan. However, most of the rest of the wall is only 6 to 8 feet wide. The western portion of the wall was first made of **turf**, a block of soil and tangled grass roots carved out of the ground. This material was probably used because there was not enough stone available in the surrounding area. However, the turf was replaced with stone in later years.

stones used to build Hadrian's Wall

The workers dug a V-shaped ditch on the north side of the wall. On the south side, they constructed the vallum, which consisted of a central ditch with a mound of earth on each side. The V-shaped ditch and the vallum both ran the entire length of the wall except in front of the gateways. This meant that people could only get through the wall at the gateway.

cross section of Hadrian's Wall

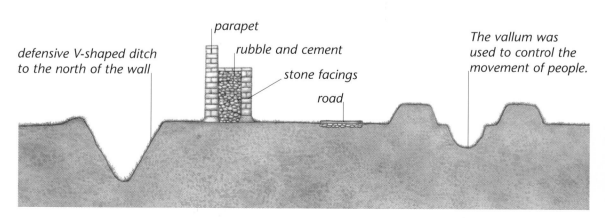

defensive V-shaped ditch to the north of the wall

parapet

rubble and cement

stone facings

road

The vallum was used to control the movement of people.

With so many soldiers coming into the area to live and work, Hadrian's Wall meant the local tradespeople had more business. Small towns developed near the forts. Local men became soldiers, and the Roman soldiers sometimes married local women. When the Roman empire lost power and moved out of northern England around A.D. 400, the local people moved into the forts and mile castles and made them their homes.

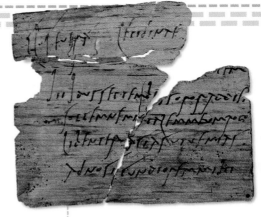

The Romans wrote about daily life at Hadrian's Wall on thin tablets of wood.

Although only crumbled ruins remain of Hadrian's Wall today, people can see reconstructions of the wall at Vindolanda, a museum that is named after a fort south of Hadrian's Wall. At this museum, visitors can see the ruins of the fort, a civilian town, and a reconstructed section of the stone and turf wall. The fort at Vindolanda is an important site where archaeologists have found many objects that give colorful details of everyday life around Hadrian's Wall.

Forts, such as this one at the Vindolanda Museum, usually included a granary for food storage, sleeping quarters, an officers' residence, a temple, stables, and sometimes a hospital.

The Berlin Wall

Berlin

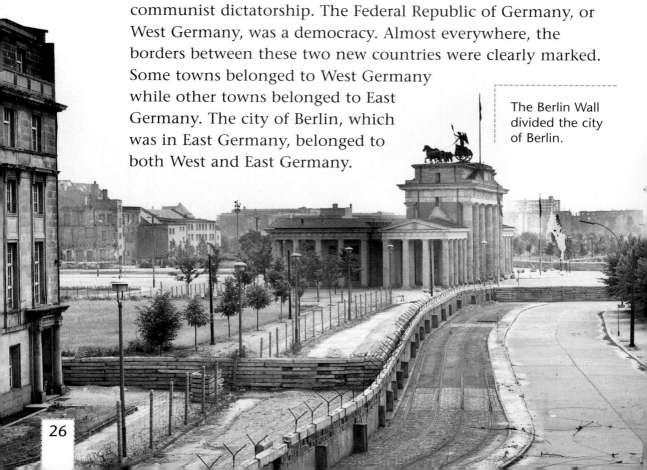

East Berlin

West Berlin

Berlin Wall

Berlin

East Germany

West Germany

The site of the Berlin Wall

Imagine if the town or city where you live was suddenly split in two by an enormous wall. This is exactly what happened when the Berlin Wall was built in 1961, dividing the East and West halves of the German city of Berlin. The wall was 12 feet high and nearly 100 miles long, and cut through neighborhoods, streets, and even buildings.

In 1949, after World War II, Germany was divided into two countries. The United Kingdom, France, and the United States were to control part of the country, and the Soviet Union was to control the rest. The German Democratic Republic, commonly known as East Germany, was a tightly controlled communist dictatorship. The Federal Republic of Germany, or West Germany, was a democracy. Almost everywhere, the borders between these two new countries were clearly marked. Some towns belonged to West Germany while other towns belonged to East Germany. The city of Berlin, which was in East Germany, belonged to both West and East Germany.

The Berlin Wall divided the city of Berlin.

This division of what had once been a single country into two meant people could no longer travel freely from one part of the country to another. Families and friends were separated, and people in both countries were sad and angry. To make matters worse, while West Germans enjoyed good living conditions, East Germans endured poverty, shortages of basic needs, and a harsh government.

Berlin was the only real pathway between the two countries because it was hard to stop people going from one place to another in a single city. Between 1949 and 1961, despite strict East German controls, nearly 3 million East Germans escaped through Berlin into West Germany hoping for a better life. The people who escaped included doctors, teachers, and engineers. So many people left East Germany that it became hard for the government to find enough workers to perform necessary jobs. East Germany's answer to the problem was to erect a wall around West Berlin.

As conditions worsened, East Germans waited in lines for hours in the hope of being able to buy basic necessities.

On August 13, 1961, East German soldiers worked in the middle of the night to erect a barbed wire barrier that was very quickly set into a concrete wall. Buildings in the way of the wall were simply bricked up to become, in a way, part of the wall itself. People in Berlin woke up and found that their city had been divided in two.

Over the years, it became harder and harder for people to get from East to West Berlin. It was even difficult to talk to relatives who lived on the other side of the wall.

The few openings in the wall were heavily guarded, as was the entire East German side of the wall. Only diplomats and foreign visitors were allowed to cross from one part of the city to the other. Armed soldiers and attack dogs patrolled the wall 24 hours a day. Deep trenches were dug to prevent cars and trucks from trying to ram through the wall. In addition to foot soldiers on the ground, the wall was constantly watched by soldiers from 20 bunkers and 302 watchtowers.

Checkpoint Charlie was one of the few places where people could officially leave East Germany.

People did not stop trying to escape from East Germany, but those who did paid a terrible price in the 1960s and 1970s. About 200 people were shot and injured trying to get across, and 192 were killed on the wall. The East German government continued to strengthen and rebuild the wall throughout the years.

Guards rebuilt the East German side of the Berlin Wall after it was rammed with a bulldozer in an escape attempt.

By 1989, the political situation in Eastern Europe was changing. People were finally free to protest about the way their governments were run. Mass demonstrations began in East Germany in September, 1989. By October, the East German head of state was forced to resign. On November 9 at 6:53 p.m., a member of the new East German government announced that travel restrictions between East and West Germany were being lifted immediately.

Thousands of people began storming the wall, cheerfully demolishing whole sections. So the wall that went up during one terrible night also began to come down in one night.

West German civilians enthusiastically attacked the Berlin Wall.

People on both sides of the Berlin Wall were overjoyed at the wall's destruction.

Official destruction of what was left of the wall began in June 1990 and was completed by November 30, 1990, except for six sections which were left standing as memorials. In Berlin, only red painted lines or double rows of cobblestones show where the wall once stood.

In October of 1990, East and West Germany were officially united into one country once again. Concrete that was part of the wall was crushed and used to build new roads for people to travel freely to places that had been restricted. Other pieces of the wall were auctioned to raise money for the reconstruction of the city, and some pieces were placed in museums. A wall that had been a symbol of terror and oppression for nearly 30 years had been reclaimed by its people and put to important new uses.

Conclusion

All of the walls featured in this book have been built to serve a certain purpose. Some have fallen or have been taken apart, but many are still in use today. By examining walls, the reasons they were built, and the materials and methods used to build them, we can gain glimpses into the minds of people who lived in the past.

Glossary

archaeologists   people who study the past by examining old objects

citizens   people who live in a town or country

dynasty   a series of rulers from the same family

emperor   the ruler of an empire

empire   a group of nations under the rule of one person or country

facings   the outside of a wall that sandwiches the core

foundation   the solid base of a wall or building

inherited   received from an ancestor

masonry   the use of stone or brick for construction

moat   a deep ditch, usually filled with water, designed to keep intruders out

monuments   buildings, statues, towers, or other structures built to honor a person or people

mortar   the material used between bricks or stones to hold them in place

parapet   a low wall or elevation to protect soldiers

turf   a surface layer of grass and earth

vallum   a Roman defensive ditch

Index